STEVE PARISH

INSPIRED BY NATURE

contents

This book is dedicated to the late Big Bill Neidjie, respected leader of the Bunitj clan of the Gagudju community of Kakadu, a man who inspired so many Balanda to understand what it means to "feel for country" from an Aboriginal perspective.

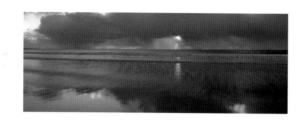

THE INSPIRATION

THE QUEST

Pages 2–3: Millaa Millaa Falls, Atherton Tableland, Queensland.

Page 7: Coneflower; eucalypt leaf; grasses and pea flowers.

Pages 8–9: Grass-tree, Flinders Ranges, South Australia.

THE STRUGGLE

THE PRODUCTION

THE CONNECTION

I am fascinated by the relationship the human race has with Nature. It inspires an entire spectrum of emotions and behaviours. Here, I have focused on those that pertain to creative endeavour, ranging from the love of animals to fear of unknown places, from seeing subtle intricate pattern through confronting obstacles to revealing a story, and then from testing imagination to the fulfilment of completing a piece of creative work.

I hold the conviction that creativity is the very essence of who we are as sentient beings, and I believe the natural world can provide our creativity with powerful stimuli. In publishing this book, I have selected photographs of subjects that have quickened my senses with their extraordinary beauty, and have written, from my personal experiences, of the profound effect the natural world can have on the human spirit.

The book is structured in chapters and episodes of inspiration, quest, struggle and the production of creative work. That done, I felt that a final chapter was necessary – the need to tell stories, to connect with others. It has been a driving force in my life. This story is told from my personal viewpoint but I know my creative journey has threads in common with many people. The urge to change something, the finding of what it is, the struggle to do it, the joy of getting there and then the sharing, lead to personal fulfilment.

I know I have grown enormously through the creation of this book and I do trust that it provides enrichment and stimulus for your creative self.

Steve Parish
Brisbane, 2004

solitude

contemplation

perception

awe

understanding

disappointment

Nature's shifting light that paints the Earth in ever-changing colours, patterns and textures can be the inspiration for taking that great leap into a creative outpouring. It can be the catalyst for an idea, as yet unformed, to crystallise into a creative vision.

This chapter is about the inspiration Nature can give, about taking the time to experience a spirit uplifted and fulfilled.

Places of solitude can inspire creativity as the senses revel in their wild beauty. Opening the mind in contemplative thought offers a pathway to enhanced perception of the natural world, to gradually see things, hear sounds, smell odours and feel textures which otherwise may have gone unnoticed. A feeling of awe results as sharpened senses bring new understandings.

Inspiration from the world of Nature seems to create a source of energy that is of enormous support in dealing with life's successes and disappointments.

Opposite: Cool temperate seas gently surge across a smooth sandy beach, a gentle breeze caresses skin, wet sand oozes between toes, soft hissing sounds of salt water soaking into fine sand meld with the cries of seabirds, and thunder rumbles in the distance — the inspiration for another day of creative play.

A stormy morning, Great Ocean Road, Victoria.

Inspiration

solitude

The monotony of a quiet life stimulates the creative mind.

Albert Einstein – scientist, philosopher

In solitude, clarity of mind comes more easily. The distractions of daily life are diminished and the sheer impact of aloneness in a wild place invites the imagination to run free. Then inspiration can develop and take form.

Sunrise, Heron Island, Great Barrier Reef Marine Park and World Heritage Area, Queensland.

Following pages: Over thousands of years the spirit of Uluṟu has been a cultural inspiration for Aṉangu communities, the traditional custodians of Uluṟu. More recently, people from the four corners of the Earth have travelled to experience the inspirational solitude of this remarkable wild place.

Uluṟu, Uluṟu–Kata Tjuṯa National Park, Northern Territory.

To enter the Fan Palm forests of tropical north Queensland is to enter the world of the Cassowary, a giant flightless bird that feeds on the nuts and fruits littering the forest floor. An encounter with one of these birds is a very special experience.

Deep inside these cathedral-like forests, the space is filled with bird-song, the pulsing sounds of insects and the rustling of the wind in the paper-like palms. To even further delight the senses, on a sunny day there is the constant interplay of light and shifting shadows against vivid green foliage.

Endangered Fan Palm Forest and a Southern Cassowary portrait, Mission Beach, Tropical North Queensland.

contemplation

Art is contemplation. It is the pleasure of the mind which searches into nature and which there divines the spirit of which nature herself is animated.

Auguste Rodin – sculptor

Contemplation can create a receptive state of mind in which the floating seed of an idea may germinate. The Sacred Lotus inspires contemplation of its beauty, reflected in still waters. Over the aeons, it has appeared in ancient Egyptian and Indian religions as a revered symbol of the Sun, creation and rebirth. In ancient Persia, it was held to have life-affirming powers.

Sacred Lotus, Kakadu National Park, Northern Territory.

Floating on the shimmering abstractions of a water-world mirror,
the Freckled Duck appears the embodiment of tranquil contemplation.

The endangered Freckled Duck, Lakes District, Victoria.

Wild places empower the mind to reach new levels of thought that fire the imagination. Awakening at dawn to see the mirror surface of an outback lagoon perfectly reflecting the sky propels the mind into a responsive state.

Hoods Lagoon, Clermont, Queensland.

perception

It is the function of art to renew our perception.

What we are familiar with we cease to see.

Anaïs Nin – author, diarist

Breathe the pungent odour of rotting kelp; feel the warm sun and the texture of sun-baked kelp fronds on naked skin; hear seal pups cry out to their returning mothers then watch as they thrill at her gentle touch – to revel in the sensory experiences of the natural world is to heighten perceptions and stimulate the mind.

Australian Fur-seal and pup, Kangaroo island, South Australia.

Free the body, mind and heart to be alive to the sound of the waves crashing on the rocks, the feel of the sea-spray misting over the skin and the sight of the glint of tiny crystals in the rocks reflecting the setting Sun.

Leeuwin–Naturaliste National Park, Western Australia.

Right: A hot day ends with a soft, cool breeze. As the Sun falls below the horizon, the distant ranges take on a purple hue and the giant River Red Gums, moments earlier stark creamy-white against the blue sky, soften as the colours of the bark shift through shades of tan to burnished gold. Sulphur-crested Cockatoos flock into the gorge to roost in the gums after feeding on the plains and begin to squabble over favoured roosting sites. All around the pulsing shrill of thousands of cicadas fades, and, in the distance, the soft thump of a wallaroo is heard as it descends from the ranges to drink.

Flinders Ranges, South Australia.

Previous pages: There are few sensory experiences in nature to rival a forest shrouded in mist. The sights, sounds, smells and feelings are muted in an intense and stirring atmosphere.

A misty forest, Yarra Ranges National Park, Victoria.

Following pages: Where the ocean washes the shore is another of nature's most inspiring locales. Sea sounds and salty air give the world a new perspective, different from anywhere else on Earth.

Bay of Fires, Mount William National Park, Tasmania.

awe

The most beautiful experience we can have is the mysterious. Whoever does not know it and can no longer wonder, no longer marvel, is as good as dead, and his eyes are dimmed.

Albert Einstein – scientist, philosopher

Encounters with nature's creations – creatures of infinite variety, exquisite flora and dramatic landscapes – can be enthralling. A sense of awe inspires the questions: Where did you come from? Where are you going? What secrets do you carry?

Manta Rays, off Lady Elliot Island, Great Barrier Reef Marine Park and World Heritage Area, Queensland.

Nature is fascinating and complex. The aesthetic appeal of its colours, patterns, shapes and forms is truly inspiring, and nowhere more so than in the ocean's depths. To glide weightlessly down stairways of shafting light, alighting gently on the bottom is to live the fantasy.

Pyrites Coral, Great Barrier Reef Marine Park and World Heritage Area, Queensland.

Harsh stony deserts, flower-covered dunes, rolling grassy knolls and plains, cascading tropical rivers, palm-filled forests, long white sandy beaches and endless ocean depths all overflow with living things. To value their complexity, appreciating their art and revelling in their gifts, can only enhance the quality of life.

Australian habitats, desert to sea.

The Proteaceae family provides colour, shape, texture and pattern sufficient for a lifetime of creative adventure.

Proteaceae from Western Australia.

understanding

Look deep, deep into nature, and then you will understand everything better.

Albert Einstein – scientist, philosopher

Knowledge enhances understanding, and a better informed eye is a discerning eye. Knowledge of frogs' distribution and behaviour leads to more purposeful observation. Understanding that their sensitivity to environmental change, particularly air and water quality, may provide early warning indicators as to the health of a wild place is inspiring.

Green Tree-frog, Mount Glorious, Brisbane, Queensland.

The journey to understanding in nature can act as a guide and motivator as the learning leads deeper into a habitat, with an invitation to stay longer, search more diligently and listen more intently.

Liffey Falls State Reserve, Tasmanian Wilderness World Heritage Area.

Above: To have some understanding of the 190,000 year geological history of the amazing Undara Lava Tubes certainly enhances the sense of drama these landscape structures engender. Their age is awesome, but the fact that some of the tubes extend 160 kilometres (100 miles), making them the longest lava flows from a single volcano on our planet, is astonishing.

Undara Volcanic National Park, eastern Gulf Savannah, north Queensland.

Opposite: This ancient coral reef is several hundred kilometres from the existing coastline – a staggering fact in a geological history that goes back so far that it is difficult to comprehend.

Boab tree in the ancient Devonian Reef country of the Kimberley, Western Australia.

disappointment

Who knows where inspiration comes from. Perhaps it arises from desperation.
Perhaps it comes from the flukes of the universe, the kindness of the muses.

Amy Tan – author

The conviction that it is possible to make a difference, particularly with young people, to share experiences and promote the health of the natural world can itself be a driving force towards a positive outlook. The depressing sight of the poor state of some parts of the environment can be the inspiration to turn that disappointment into motivation for action through education.

I have spent more than twenty years recording the pockets of Australia's old growth forests on film before they disappear.
It is a great disappointment – shared by many Australians and expressed in many ways – that these living treasures are daily
being reduced to giant scars on land once rich in old growth forest ecosystems.

Above: The Styx Valley, on the doorstep of the Tasmanian Wilderness World Heritage Area.
Top right: Road sign, Tasmania. *Bottom right:* The aftermath.

While the Pig-nosed Turtle was well known to Aboriginal communities of western Arnhem Land – around Kakadu National Park – science, knowing only of its presence in the area through rock art, had recorded this reptile as extinct. During a workshop in 1980, trainee Aboriginal Rangers volunteered the information that the reptile was alive and thriving in its remaining wild habitat of pristine rivers and streams. The turtle is now under threat in the Alligator River system from habitat degradation.

Opposite page: Nourlangie Rock and Anbangbang Billabong, Kakadu National Park, Northern Territory.
Left and above: Underwater photographs of the curious Pig-nosed Turtle and the crystal clear waters that are its home.

journeying

desire

choice

imagination

determination

seeing

patience

Most of life is a quest. Goals may change as the search for a path progresses – indeed, goal posts may be moved by unforeseeable circumstances – but the exploration for purpose, relevance and happiness, involving self, others, lifestyle, and creativity goes on and, fortunately, self-knowledge evolves. Dead-ends, side-roads and unexpected corners will test vision, imagination and patience to the limit. Reflecting on the emotions released may expand the limits of personal expression.

On the questing journey, change can appear to be a threat. Fear may bite hard, especially when the change in direction is toward an unknown future. There is always the possibility that the passage of time will reveal that the thing most feared was the greatest contributor to the enhancement of our existence. These difficult times will require determination and a strong desire to prevail. Yet, all along the way we must remind ourselves to appreciate the challenge of the quest as much as the pursuit of the outcome.

Opposite: A winding, dusty back-road has its own journey and destination.

Flinders Ranges National Park, South Australia.

journeying

The journey from the familiar to new places, experiences and ideas may lead to increased self-awareness and expanded horizons. It may be undertaken in the mind, or physically.

The tracks of an Eastern Quoll in sand – a small event and an ephemeral record, yet one of my journey's rewards considering these small marsupials are all but extinct on the mainland.

Bay of Fires, Mount William National Park, Tasmania.

Revisiting well known landscapes is seldom a wasted journey. At a different time of day or year, the light, the colours and the moods will be different; from a different viewpoint, new natural beauties may be revealed; you will be seeing with new eyes. While looking through my photographic collection and remembering my life at the time, I can see the changes in my attitude reflected in my work. In effect, the collection is a visual record of my self and my many journeys.

Liffey Falls State Reserve, Tasmanian Wilderness World Heritage Area, Tasmania.

Taking time for adventuring and the new experiences it offers can lead to a clearer thinking about life, choices and priorities. Shark Bay, where red desert sands meet glistening white beaches that tumble into the aqua blue Indian Ocean, is a unique, wild and remote place. A World Heritage Area of national and marine parks, it fills the heart and mind, and brings a special joy to the journey.

Above: The wild seacoast near Steep Point, the most westerly point of Australia's land mass, Shark Bay, Western Australia.
Opposite: Cape Peron North, Shark Bay World Heritage Area, Western Australia.

Coral sea islands are evocative wild places. Because of their remoteness from the hustle and bustle of everyday life, they are the sorts of places that make it easy to escape into the world of Nature, particularly during the summer months when the breezes are warm and the weather is balmy.

During a summer visit, you are likely to encounter two of Nature's more impressive examples of animals that make remarkable journeys, marine turtles and boobies. Turtles may migrate thousands of kilometres from feeding to nesting grounds. Boobies fly long distances each day in search of food, and hunt by diving vertically from heights of up to 100 metres, plunging deep underwater.

Left: Sunrise on Heron Island, Great Barrier Reef, Queensland.
Above, top to bottom: A Brown Booby and a Green Turtle, Great Barrier Reef, Queensland.

desire

*Art is the desire of a man to express himself, to record
the reactions of his personality to the world he lives in.*

Amy Lowell – poet

The desire to embark on a quest, an irresistible longing to explore, can be the catalyst for life change. It might start with the kernel of an idea and come to mind from time to time. When you lie awake at night planning and visualising then wake in the morning thinking about it, seize the moment and run with the feelings!

Left: Porcupine Gorge National Park, central Queensland. *Above:* Designed by Nature. Bay of Fires, Mount William National Park, Tasmania.

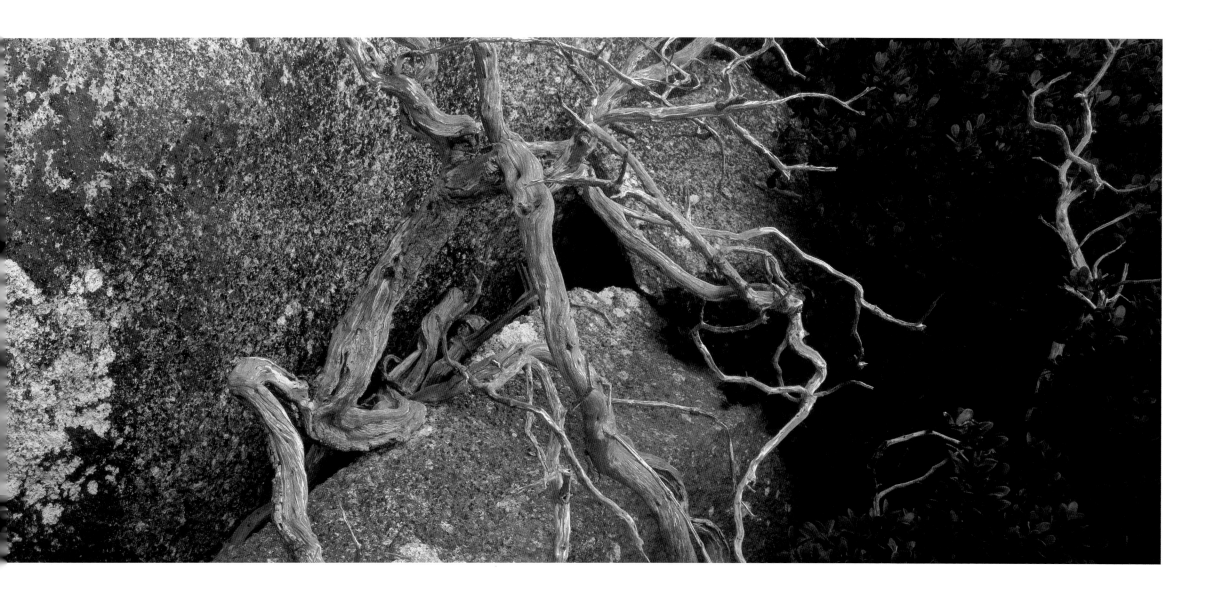

As human beings, it is no longer enough for us simply to desire to enjoy Nature's bounty; we have to ensure its continuing presence in our world.

Ian Morris – naturalist

Desire is usually unplanned and unexpected, and manifests itself through a sense of special connection with the object of desire. This intense focused emotion can be overwhelming but it provides a great sense of purpose.

Above, left to right: The Eastern Quoll, and one of its habitats, highland heath in Tasmania.

People cannot be expected to care about animals they cannot connect to because of the creatures' rarity or their habits. It has long been my desire to make that connection possible through my photographic and publishing work.

For the Eastern Quoll, which has all but disappeared from the mainland, and the Spectacled Flying Fox, their continued survival is under threat. For both, habitat clearing is an issue, as are introduced plants and animals.

Above, left to right: Its rainforest habitat, Daintree, Queensland, and the Spectacled Flying-fox.

choice

We must make the choices that enable us to fulfil the deepest capacities of our real selves.

Thomas Merton – writer, monk

The choices of everyday life are many. A wise choice usually requires thoughtful deliberation, but sometimes a heartfelt connection means there is really no choice at all except what the heart dictates. The challenges of responsible choice can be fearsome and outcomes unexpected. Taking up those challenges mindful of the implications increases the chances of managed and beneficial outcomes.

Mottlecah, south-west Western Australia.

It was a chance encounter with the Mottlecah's spectacular blossom some years back that inflamed my passion for wildflower image making and, later, I chose to take up video photography to capture their beauty in motion.

The Mottlecah, largest of the eucalypt flowers, south-west Western Australia.

Will I? Won't I? Every one of the myriad choices faced each day can have far-reaching consequences.

Above and opposite: Australian Pelicans, Stradbroke Island, Queensland.

imagination

Imagination is the playground of the mind. It knows no bounds. It will take you, in your mind's eye, wherever your heart desires. It can be fed and extended by visualisation and freeing the mind to journey where it will. Work on self awareness can also release the fetters on the imagination and allow it to soar.

The colours of sunrise at the beach, Port Douglas, Tropical North Queensland.

The rising and setting of the Sun trigger enormous activity in Nature, particularly in the tropics.
They are the times when the specialised creatures of the day and night seek rest or food.
Given such fuel for inspiration, the imagination sets to work.

Magpie Geese leaving the floodplain at dusk, Town Common, Townsville, Queensland.

One of the greatest joys of my life was when I realised that my imagination, which has been developing over time, had started to work in new and exciting ways. Ideas began to flow where once there were blockages. It is like finding a new best friend and then going on the most amazing trips together.

Beyond imagination in the Top End, Northern Territory.
Opposite: Tropical Pandanus palms and floodplain.
Above: A Varied Lorikeet.

determination

Redirect the substantial energy of your frustration and turn it into positive, effective, unstoppable determination.

Ralph Marston – motivator

Despite our best efforts and intentions, when the going gets really tough we all flirt with giving up on our dreams. Doing something just for you – something as simple as framing and hanging a photograph you have taken, one you think is good – may provide the self-affirming impetus to get your confidence and energy back to pursue your goals.

Twilight over subtropical woodland, Bunya Mountains National Park, Queensland.

Any creative endeavour requires determination. It is all too easy to give up during the early stages when new skills may need to be mastered or new paths trodden. If the goal is achievable, the desire is unquenched, the inspiration is undimmed, and the determination to succeed is strong, the quest will be accomplished.

Backlit gum leaves, Victoria.

It takes a lot of determination to get more than a couple of worthwhile images of the Platypus. Like most wild creatures it will not perform to order, and slips beneath the surface of its watery habitat and out of sight at the least provocation.

Left: Mossman River, Mossman Gorge National Park, Queensland.
Above: Platypus, Broken River, Eungella National Park, Queensland.

Following pages: Here, at the south-west corner of Australia at a delightful place called Cape Leeuwin, I was determined to come away with a series of special images but was anxious about fickle weather. While I was waiting for a break in the weather, the thought occurred to me that the 17th century Dutch mariners on the *Leeuwin* knew the true meaning of determination. The conditions they had to endure would have tested the strongest nerves. Their choices were stay determined or die! Then suddenly a shaft of light caught the foreground and the lighthouse buildings.

Cape Leeuwin Lighthouse, south-west Western Australia.

seeing

What is art but a way of seeing?

Saul Bellow – author, biographer

What am I doing but recording what my eye can see? No two people see the same thing in the same way – each brings personal interpretation to what is seen. The only way I can push my limits is to learn more, use what I learn to gain new understandings, and see in new ways.

Above, left to right: Wet season runoff, and raindrops pooling in a lotus lily leaf, Kakadu National Park, Northern Territory.

 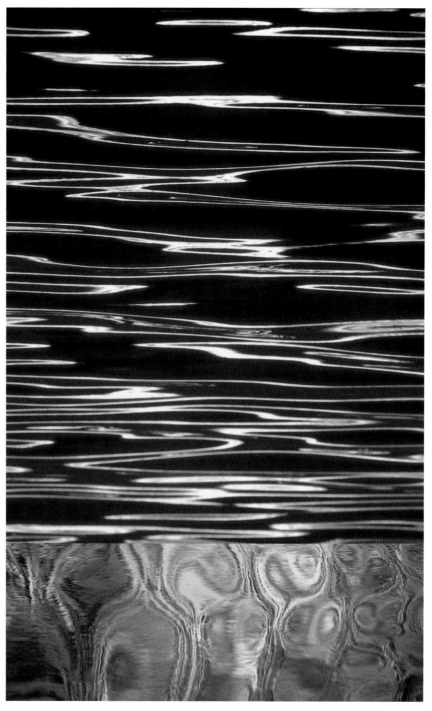

Striking designs are everywhere in Nature. It is a world that abounds with shape, pattern, texture and colour. Ways of seeing can be developed through research – the more you know about a subject, the more there is to see and interpret; experimentation – the more you practice, the more you can focus on the subject rather than the technique; and awareness – the sharper your eye, the more accomplished the result.

Left to right: Frog and palm shadows, Queensland; water reflections, Western Australia.

While the drama of aesthetically presented shapes, patterns and textures abound in the micro world; they also occur in the landscape. This rock is actually about twelve metres wide, yet the severe cropping of visual information that might assist recognition – it is actually part of a very familiar landscape structure that has been seen by thousands – adds mystery to the image. The positioning of a striking blue sky, the dark shadow balanced by the rock texture and colour add tension making the image appealing.

Above: A section of the Remarkable Rocks, Flinders Chase National Park, Kangaroo Island, South Australia.

In any landscape, everywhere are individual graphic designs that can be isolated from the whole by the practised eye. This is particularly true of rocky country. In the image of Uluṟu (opposite, bottom), the elements that draw the eye are the contrasts in the light and shade, the colours, and the shapes as seen in the discipline of the rock and the confusion of the tree. The image of Mount Buffalo (opposite, top), focuses more on the hard lines of the black rock silhouetted against the softness of distant ranges and a sky full of colour.

Opposite, top: Mount Buffalo National Park, Victoria. *Opposite, bottom:* Uluṟu, Uluṟu – Kata Tjuṯa National Park, Northern Territory.

To find and photograph these orchids from south-west Western Australia, the eye has to be educated to their presence. They are startlingly beautiful but, in the wild, their fine shapes merge with the grasses of their surrounds. As time passes, the eye "tunes in" and they become easier to discern. Once a specimen is found, it is necessary to switch from the functional search mode to the aesthetic, and enjoy and record its delicate beauty.

Left to right from opposite: Talbot's Spider Orchid, Clubbed Spider Orchid, Coastal Spider Orchid, Pink Fairy Orchid, Custard Orchid, Queen of Sheba.

Camouflage is a game we all like to play, but our secrets are as surely revealed by what we want to seem to be as by what we want to conceal.

Russell Lynes – author

Some wild creatures are masters of optical illusion. They are superbly adapted to their habitat and habits, their form, patterns and colours providing camouflage from predators when they are at rest and camouflaging them from their prey when they are hunting. Finding these sorts of animals in the wild takes an educated eye, patience and knowledge of their habitat and behaviour.

Above: Cairns Birdwing Butterfly, tropical rainforest, north Queensland.
Opposite: Lionfish, Great Barrier Reef Marine Park and World Heritage Area, Queensland.

patience

Adopt the pace of nature: her secret is patience.

Ralph Waldo Emerson – poet, philosopher

What we cannot control, we must learn to accept, particularly in Nature. There is no point in chasing after a wild creature or cursing the rain. Learn that it is better to wait patiently and unnoticed, or that the clarity of the sky after rain is unparalleled. Patience and deliberation need not stifle inspiration, merely adapt it to prevailing conditions.

Above and opposite: Sacred Kingfisher and mangrove trees, Dunk Island, Queensland.

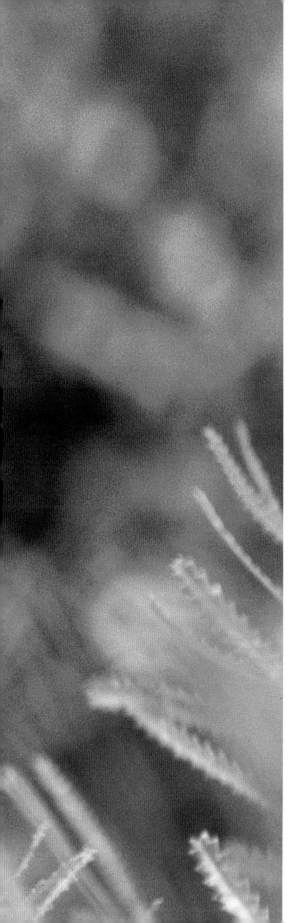

Often I return from a trip with an entirely different set of pictures from what I envisioned because the prevailing conditions dictated that I change my plans. Then my only course of action is to relax into the environment and be patient with my quarry. The results may be surprisingly good when we are tolerant, patient and accepting and not stressed by feeling that we need to control an outcome.

Above: Constantly alert for their own safety, to defend their territory and during the egg laying season, little bush birds move with alarming speed, and only extreme patience brings rewarding images.

Superb Fairy-wren, Victoria.

Opposite: Patience is rewarded – a honeyeater called after Australia's first European name alights on a flower named for the botanist on Cook's first voyage to Australia, Joseph Banks.

New Holland Honeyeater on a banksia flower, South Australia.

Following pages: With only about thirty-two fine days each year and even fewer sunny days, Cradle Mountain is one landscape where photographers need to practise considerable patience to capture shafts of sunlight over the lake and mountain.

Cradle Mountain–Lake St Clair National Park, Tasmania.

THE STRUGGLE

permission

time

tension

change

frustration

suspense

discovery

anticipation

Part of the challenge of doing something that is just for you, such as taking up a creative pastime, is giving yourself the permission to do it. Taking this course will certainly affect your daily life. There may be a need to examine and reset priorities. Issues that arise with those who share your world may have to be negotiated: after all, the chosen path may be costly in money, space and time. Taking time to explore the new-found creative self, along with the acceptance of new kinds of tension, change and disappointments in life, will all become part of the struggle.

The good news is that, over time and with patience and tolerance, the struggle, whether physical or emotional, becomes easier to deal with. There are times when the path to resolution is not clear and sometimes the accompanying frustration seems overwhelming. However, once your life adapts to its new rhythms, exciting possibilities and discoveries may lead to paths that were once beyond your imagination.

When dreams become reality, the rewards will make all the effort worthwhile. Struggle is part of what it is to be human. Without struggle there would be no development of self, no increased awareness, and no broadening of creative endeavours.

Opposite: Do you ever feel that you are the only one going your way?

One-spot Puller, Lord Howe Island, New South Wales.

The Struggle

permission

If you think you can, you can.

And if you think you can't, you're right.

old saying

Creative self-realisation is often not a comfortable state to be in. You can give yourself many excuses for not taking the journey: "No time. No money. Can't." To allow the processes of development to begin, make the time, accept the consequences, be brave in creative expression, and believe and trust in yourself.

Above: A school of pike formed a swirling defensive pod to confuse predatory Barracuda. I lay on my back on the sea floor and angled my camera towards the sun. It was a surreal experience and I created this montage to capture something of that.

Opposite: I was so absorbed with the textures and colours of a Wedge-tailed Eagle's feathers that, rather than remain in my normal illustrative frame of mind, I gave myself permission to experiment with the images.

Following a creative dream can be a challenge, but is always spiritually and mentally worthwhile. In the mid 1990s, I bought a digital video camera and followed the wildflower bloom down the west coast and into the centre of Australia's vast deserts. Filming Australia's fascinating wildflowers was my motive, but I had no particular outcome in mind – I had always just wanted the time to wander.

Above: Sturt's Desert Pea, Parakeelya and Showy Eremophila.
Opposite: Kata Tjuṯa, Uluṟu–Kata Tjuṯa National Park, Northern Territory.

time

They say that time changes things, but you actually have to change them yourself.

Andy Warhol – artist

Making time for creative passions is a challenge given the demands of modern life. But how sad it would be to grow old with dreams unfulfilled. The time to plan and manage your priorities and maintain a balanced lifestyle equates to mere moments in the timescale written in the ancient landscapes. Overall, time for creative play and contemplative reflection is time well spent.

Three Sisters, Blue Mountains National Park, New South Wales.

The story of the ages is recorded in the rocks of ancient landscapes, making our brief visit to this planet seem little more than a fleeting moment in time. The rock in the cliff face above originated as sediment on the sea floor around 2500 million years ago, whereas the sediment of the Three Sisters was laid down over a mere 250 million years.

Hamersley Gorge, Karijini National Park, Western Australia.

In the feathers of the "living dinosaurs" can be read the struggle for survival over the aeons.
Birds are creatures of exquisite design, superb engineering and efficient construction.
Most of them are capable of what humans can do only in dreams – flight. In their many and
varied ways of life and behaviours, they have always fascinated people and brought us joy.

Feathers discarded and on living birds, recorded in Queensland, Victoria and the Northern Territory.

Australia is rich in native fauna, and, of land invertebrates, reptiles have the most species. They are an intriguing group of animals in how they fit in to their habitats, the ways they move and their lifestyles. This montage of images came together when I took the time to play with images. Reptile colours, skin textures and scale patterning are collectively the stuff of art.

Snake, gecko and crocodile skin colours and textures photographed on living animals in Queensland and the Northern Territory.

tension

The world is all gates, all opportunities, strings of tension waiting to be struck.

Ralph Waldo Emerson – poet, philosopher

Tension originates either externally or internally, usually a combination of the two. It may heighten awareness, sharpen the senses and foster a special kind of creative thinking. The trick, then, is to make it work for you and not against you, and one way to do that is to be self aware and attuned to your surroundings.

Black-headed Python, Northern Territory.

Numbats nest in hollows in fallen limbs and trunks of trees. In this particular big old tree trunk, there was a family in residence but it was a cold morning and there was no sign of movement until after the Sun had risen to produce warming rays. The ears appeared first, and then the eyes, followed by a snout. All senses were now in action. I held my breath and my heart was racing as the Numbat slowly and deliberately left its hollow and began to step very warily down the trunk.

Numbat, Earth Sanctuaries, South Australia.

It can be a pretty tense time entering the habitat of the Saltwater Crocodile on foot, wading in shallow water along the banks of billabongs, creeks and rivers. The mating season, when males are competing for supremacy and territory, and later, the egg-laying season when females are guarding their nests, are times to exercise extreme caution. Whenever you intrude on this highly successful animal's habitat, it is probably wise to maintain a healthy level of fear and respect for the Saltwater Crocodile, expert in camouflage and one of Nature's most efficient predators.

A mangrove-lined creek, perfect habitat for this large, patrolling Saltwater Crocodile in the Daintree, north Queensland.

*Conditions for creativity are to be puzzled;
to concentrate; to accept conflict and tension;
to be born everyday; to feel a sense of self.*

Erich Fromm – psychotherapist, philosopher

Left: It was a most beautiful day: cool, yet warm in the sunshine. Having little fortune in my pursuit of Rose Robins I lay back in the lush grasses and drifted off to sleep. Suddenly awake, I sensed that I was not alone. Looking back over my shoulder I saw I had a very dramatic companion. Standing tall and stock-still only a matter of metres away was a large male Eastern Grey Kangaroo. He had been standing guard over his mob of females and juveniles further back. Our momentary connection was filled with tension. One click from the camera and he was gone, his mob hot on his heels.

Eastern Grey Kangaroo, Kosciuszko National Park, New South Wales.

Opposite: As with most birds of prey, the cold, staring, hooded eyes of the Wedge-tailed Eagle seem to emanate tension. In fact this animal is in a constant state of alertness to the signals of the world in which it lives and has highly developed senses, especially eyesight. This adolescent female Wedge-tailed Eagle started its life as a deserted chick. It was hand-raised by skilled staff and used as part of the sanctuary's free flight exhibit.

Wedge-tailed Eagle, Healesville Sanctuary, Victoria.

change

Change does not roll in on the wheels of inevitability,

but comes through continuous struggle.

Martin Luther King, Jr – pastor, civil rights leader

Unseasonal weather and seismic episodes are Nature's reminders that, despite the predictability of some events, the physical world is in a constant state of flux. Change is inevitable and adaptability is one of the keys to survival. Gaining an understanding of the processes of change will also help unlock some of the spiritual aspects of life.

Uluṟu at the time of the Honey Grevillea bloom, Uluṟu–Kata Tjuṯa National Park, Northern Territory.

Spiritual change lies within our control: acceptance and management of change relate directly to creativity, personal growth and lifestyle. Conformity is often self-imposed, so learning to embrace change, to see it as a challenge, is an opportunity to make exciting discoveries.

Above: Images reflecting changing seasons in a tropical woodland, Northern Territory.
Following pages: Uluṟu looms in the background of red sand plains in bloom, Uluṟu–Kata Tjuṯa National Park, Northern Territory.

Australian woodlands are in a state of constant renewal. Seasonal rains prompt vivid green new growth that matures during drier times to grey-green foliage and golden swathes of long grass.

Left to right: The woodlands along the Scenic Rim, northern New South Wales; the Brown Falcon, reliant on the food that the seasons provide, Lawn Hill National Park, Queensland.

Australia is a continent of extremes. The baking heat of the Red Centre is a dramatic change from the soft white carpet of snow in alpine country. The stark beauties of each are inspiring, and each has its challenges.

Mount Wellington, Tasmania.

Following pages: When a familiar landscape is revisited after some time away there is a natural tendency to reflect on changes that have occurred as the years pass. How has this place changed? Am I seeing the landscape differently? How far have I come? Have I grown as a person? These and a hundred other questions flood the mind.

Heron Island, Great Barrier Reef Marine Park and World Heritage Area, Queensland.

frustration

Think not about your frustrations, but about your unfulfilled potential. Concern yourself not with what you tried and failed in, but with what it is still possible for you to do.

Pope John XXIII – spiritual leader, Catholic Church

All problem solving can be beset by frustration. The elements that provoke a reaction may well be minor and scarcely noticed by others. The best action is always to transform the energy of frustration into positive work.

The drama of Uluṟu on a stormy day, Uluṟu–Kata Tjuṯa National Park, Northern Territory.

It is interesting to observe how our moods can be affected by changes in the weather. Gloomy and wet weather, day after day, can cause negativity and depression. But positive thinking can turn an annoying wet day to great creative advantage.

A collection from wet days.

For many of the frustrations in everyday life, we find scapegoats in other people. It is usually difficult to remember that *not* to be frustrated is one of the choices. It takes a conscious effort of will, which may be a struggle, to bring to light the real source of frustration and the resolution.

Florence Falls, Litchfield National Park, Northern Territory.

suspense

This suspense is terrible. I hope it will last.

Oscar Wilde – poet, playwright

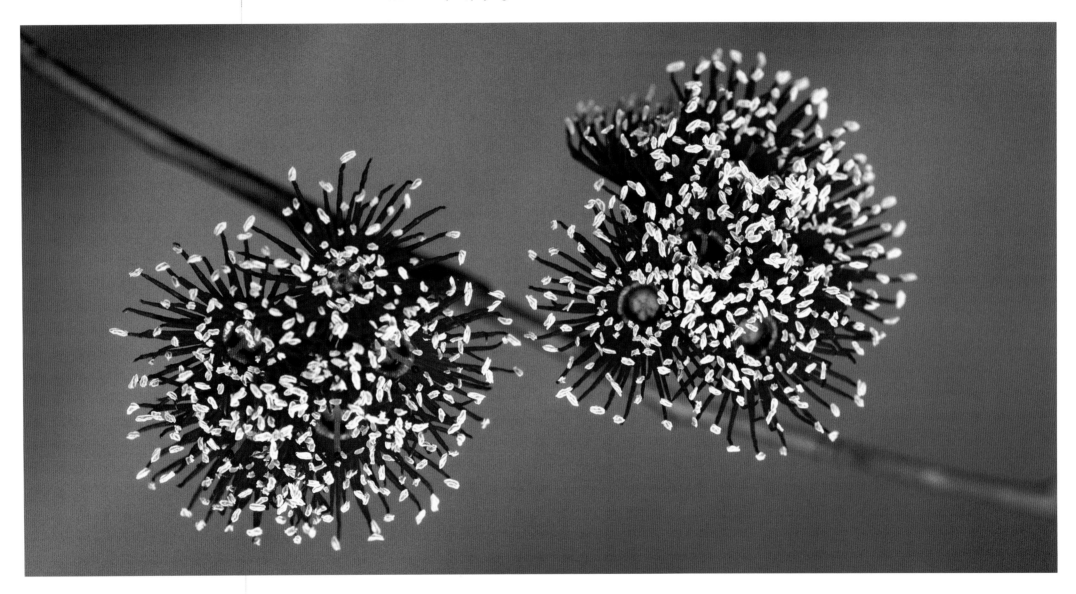

Suspense is a heightened state, teetering on the edge, almost panicked, adrenaline rushing. It should be cautiously welcomed, for in that state inspired work is possible. The mind discards distractions and focuses on solutions to problems and frustrations. Caution is needed so that balance is maintained.

A delightful crimson mallee flower, Victoria.

The thrill of struggling through wild places is allied to the suspense of not knowing what lies ahead. Will the rare and beautiful bird sit still for the shot? Is the light going to stay on those trees long enough for me to set up the tripod? Will the wildflower bloom be fresh and bright or withered and faded? It is an intoxicating experience.

Mallees glowing in the light of a setting sun, Western Australia.

Popular literature and films tend to associate suspense in the underwater world with fearsome sharks, usually White Pointers. For those who dive this world, every descent is full of excited anticipation of what discoveries might lie ahead in this largely unexplored world.

Above: A solitary, fast swimming, predatory carangid fish crossing the reef crest at high tide to feed on the slopes below, Swains Reefs, Great Barrier Reef Marine Park and World Heritage Area, Queensland.
Opposite: Panicking baitfish create a pathway for two marauding carangids, Lady Elliot Island, Great Barrier Reef Marine Park and World Heritage Area, Queensland.

In children's myth, legend, film and story, misty, dark forests are filled with danger and should be feared. Even in adulthood, the irrational mind can send a suspenseful chill down the spine as the wind sings, shadows move and leaves rustle. All Nature's moods are food for thought and inspiration.

Above: Low cloud and high sun have created this wonderful shafting light at Lamington National Park, Queensland.
Opposite: Tropical mist forest at Eungella National Park, Queensland.

discovery

The voyage of discovery is not in seeking

new landscapes but in having new eyes.

Marcel Proust – author

Making new personal discoveries, in any facet of life, is exciting, and Nature is rich with such experiences. Discovering something new to science, such as this sea-whip anemone, is a special thrill that validates effort and is a spur to further exploration and creativity.

Sea-whip anemone, photographed for the first time in 1969 in 40 metres (120 feet) of water, Point Perpendicular, Jervis Bay, New South Wales.

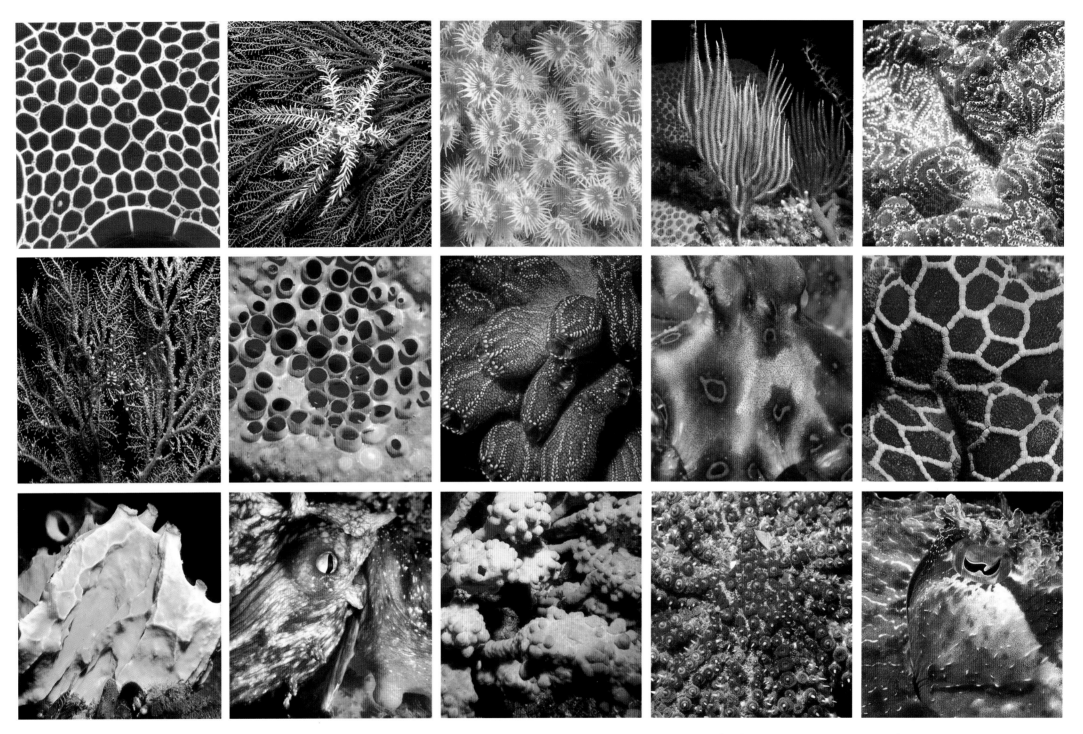

During the 1960s and 70s, the deeper southern reefs of Australia were a particular focus for scientific discovery and I was thrilled to be one of a small group pioneering the underwater photography of that "new world". Being first is wonderful for the self-esteem, and it doesn't have to be a world's first – a personal first, or best, is just as affirming.

The marvellous textures and patterns of invertebrates. Jervis Bay, New South Wales.

For many years, discovering and photographing marine creatures of the deeper waters of southern Australia was my life. In fact, I was so obsessed that every waking hour I dreamed of my next dive.

When descending the massive drop offs into deeper water, divers often encounter fish swimming up from the deep reefs, clouding around in a mass of swirling colour. As time passes, not that there is much time at these depths, the fish increase in numbers and on occasion, there were so many that the little existing light was obliterated.

Above, left to right: Patrolling Nannygai; two Knight Fish and a Bulls-eye, 55 metres (170 feet) New South Wales.
Opposite: One-spot and Splendid Perch, 55 metres (170 feet), Jervis Bay, New South Wales.

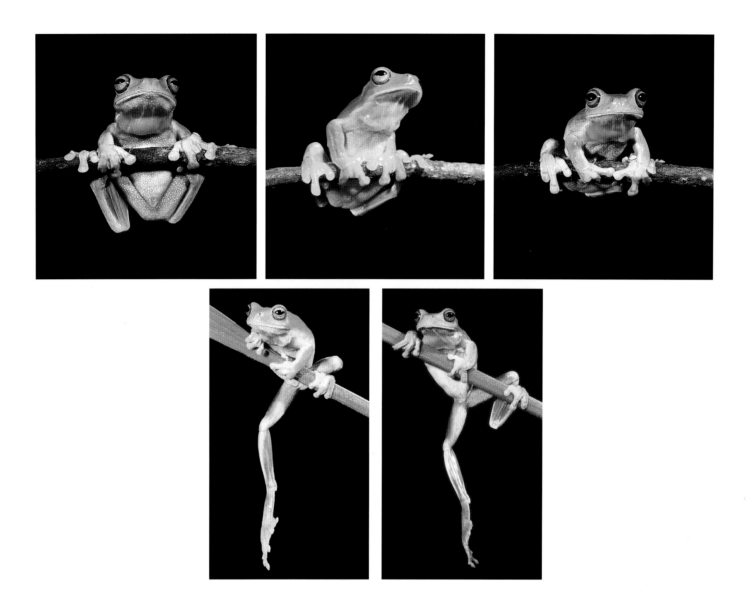

Above: Rain falls, the night is pitch black, the forest smells of rotting leaf litter. At exactly these times, thousands of frogs emerge, males calling to females: they mate and lay their eggs. For froggers, this is a time of high activity and as many as eight or ten species may be discovered in a healthy habitat.

Red-eyed Tree-frogs, south-east Queensland.

Opposite: The warm, humid atmosphere, and crystal clear cascades and streams of tropical rainforest is perfect frog habitat.

Nandroya Falls, Wooroonooran National Park, Tropical North Queensland.

Previous pages: When I learnt that the giant boulders are slowly moving downhill, they seemed to exemplify human struggle and my experience in this wild place took on a new meaning.

Mount Field National Park, Tasmania.

anticipation

Anticipation: the long, hot and dusty drive to a tropical billabong; the lift-off to soar above an impenetrable landscape; the fall backwards into deep, clear water; the journey to a remote desert region in the hope that rain will have brought the parched earth to life. Then come the moments full of potential when the billabong is swum, the landscape framed, the bush brought into focus and the dawn light metered. Will I get what I came here for? and soon the intense anticipation of possibility becomes reality.

Above and opposite: The Bungle Bungles. Purnululu National Park, the Kimberley, Western Australia.

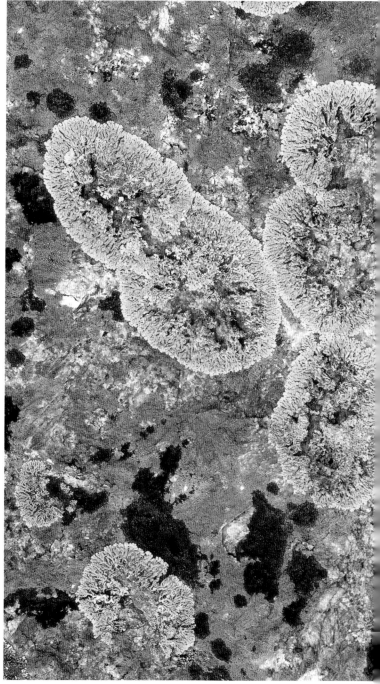

To wait excitedly is one of life's more intense sensations. That moment when the light and tide are right is magic. But it would be a mistake to ignore what is right under our feet: there are exquisite treasures to be discovered.

Above right: Three species of lichen, a colourful abstract pattern over seashore boulders, east coast Tasmania.
Above: The Hazards, Freycinet Peninsula, Tasmania.
Following pages: The Friendly Beaches, Freycinet National Park, Tasmania.
Followed by: Sunset, when more perfect conditions could not have been anticipated, Fannie Bay, Darwin.

commitment

passion

playing

designing

evaluating

failure

originality

focus

resolution

The culmination of the inspiration, the quest and the struggle is the most enthralling phase of all – the production. Problems of emotion, aesthetics and form are resolved in meeting the great challenge to produce what began as an outpouring from the heart and imagination.

The production is motivated by passion, designed through experimental play, evaluated by experience and then driven to a final resolution by a commitment to the creative self.

Each production – be it writing a music score, planting a garden bed, sewing a needlepoint sampler, arranging furniture in the office – has similar elements requiring imagination and practical skills. Each also has stages at which problems will need to be solved reflecting your truth.

The camera, the brush, the musical instrument, the pen or the computer should not drive this production: they are only the tools for an expression of your soul.

Opposite: Nature under production.

Anson Bay, Norfolk Island, 1500 kilometres off the coast of New South Wales.

commitment

Anyone can dabble, but once you've made that commitment, your blood has that particular thing in it, and it's very hard for people to stop you.

Bill Cosby – actor, comedian

All dreams, and all productions of creative work, will almost certainly encounter hurdles that seem insurmountable. If the process is driven by passion, commitment is more easily maintained. I am passionate about wildlife photography, and my commitment is to make images that capture the essence, the spirit, of the animal.

Masked Booby, Swains Reefs, Great Barrier Reef Marine Park and World Heritage Area, Queensland.

The character of the Major Mitchell's Cockatoo is less obtrusive than that of its relatives. I have tried to capture this in the portrait of a preening individual.

Major Mitchell's Cockatoo, Victoria.

Unicornfish, of the surgeonfish family, are not the easiest species to approach. This solitary individual happened to be curious enough to break from a passing school to swing by for closer inspection of this strange, bubble-blowing man-fish. I had to react quickly to produce this image.

Big-nose Unicornfish, Great Barrier Reef Marine Park and World Heritage Area, Queensland.

As though choreographed for a ballet, this small school of fish remained with me for the duration of the dive. I made many images in an attempt to capture the poetry of their squadron-like formation.

Batfish, Great Barrier Reef Marine Park and World Heritage Area, Queensland.

Commitment is the enemy of resistance, for it is the serious promise to press on, to get up, no matter how many times you are knocked down.

David McNally – business executive, motivator

Like so many animal groups, reptiles have a small yet very enthusiastic fan club. Reptile photography requires dedication because the majority of them are secretive and well camouflaged, and many are nocturnal. The rewards of a sighting in the wild are many, particularly if the observer has a camera in hand.

Above: A large male Frillneck Lizard in full breeding colours raises its crest, Northern Territory.
Opposite: A rare albino Carpet Python, Northern Territory.

passion

Love your calling with passion, it is the meaning of your life.

Auguste Rodin – sculptor

Passion provides the energy to fuel the drive to complete a creative venture, but it does need to be primed, stoked and kept afire by acquiring the knowledge that sheds light on the essence of the object of such intense emotion. I find that, when I return to the subjects which resonate in my heart – gum trees, gum blossoms and wild landscapes being three – barriers to progress dissolve.

Desert Bloodwood, Keep River National Park, Northern Territory.

Certain picturesque trees are special friends, and I try, whenever possible, to revisit them. I have photographed some individuals repeatedly over thirty years. Always, they have something new to show me.

Ghost Gum reflections in a billabong, the Pilbara, Western Australia.

The fragrance of eucalyptus carried on a summer breeze evokes a thousand memories. During spring, gum blossoms burst with vibrant colour and the drone of insects fills the air as they feed on the sweet nectar.

Gum blossoms from across Australia.

The colours, shapes and textures of Australia's ancient landscapes, when painted with our unique southern light, engender such admiration of their beauty and such sentiment that it is hard to leave. Always, they call me back.

Above, top to bottom: The Pinnacles, Nambung National Park, Western Australia;
The Bungle Bungles, Purnululu National Park, Western Australia.
Opposite, top to bottom: The Painted Desert, South Australia; The MacDonnell Ranges, South Australia.
Following pages: A detail from Gantheaume Point, Broome, Western Australia.

playing

We don't stop playing because we grow old;

we grow old because we stop playing.

George Bernard Shaw – playwright, novellist

Creativity is in us all, and it can be discovered in every facet of life. It is best accessed through play, that wonderful ability we had as children. Although the responsibilities of adulthood may have suppressed playfulness, it can be recaptured to awaken creativity.

The antics of pelicans make me laugh and I usually find photographing them puts me in a playful mood. The pelican is a favourite Australian with its mohawk hairdo and apparently humorous, animated expressions.

Above and opposite: Australian Pelicans, Narooma, New South Wales.

Whatever the subject – birds, flowers or misty forests – I find that whenever I am of a mind to play and work outside the usual constraints, it shows in the results. The images reflect the creative moment in composition, colour, shape and texture.

Above: Paper Daisies, Western Australia.
Opposite: Major Mitchell's Cockatoo, Victoria.
Following pages: Yarra Ranges National Park, Victoria.

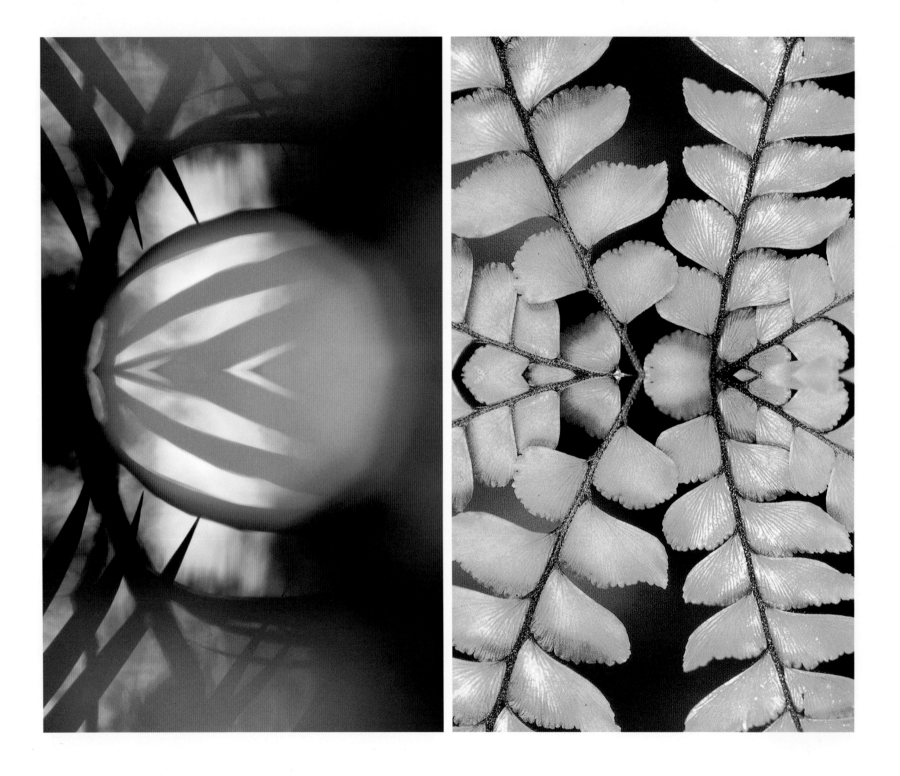

Above and opposite: The fern forests of Australian cool temperate rainforest are wonderful places to immerse yourself in creative pastimes. The soft light, gently flowing streams, cascading waterfalls, and moss covered tree trunks invigorate the senses.

Russell Falls, Mount Field National Park, Tasmania.

designing

I look for what needs to be done....

After all, that's how the universe designs itself.

R. Buckminster Fuller – inventor, architect, engineer, mathematician

Many elements exist in every setting and the story to be told is in the arrangement of the elements – the design. How well a design is executed corresponds with the story's effectiveness. When I was contemplating the image above, I was able to design it as a silhouette, emphasising the bird's hunting posture, because the shape of an egret is so appealing and easily recognised.

Above: Eastern Reef Egret, Heron Island, Queensland.
Opposite: Grass-tree detail after rain, Western Australia.

The vibrant colours, dramatic shapes and intriguing patterns found in the deep have ever commanded the attention of artists and graphic designers and elements from this world can be seen decorating utilitarian items from clothing to interior decor.

Above: Lionfish and Gorgonian Coral, Great Barrier Reef Marine Park and World Heritage Area, Queensland.
Opposite: Blue Angelfish and Gorgonian Coral, Great Barrier Reef Marine Park and World Heritage Area, Queensland.

Generally, art and design principles – colour isolation, lines, the rule of thirds, balance, space and framing – are applied to image making. However, I endorse the philosophy of the 19th century photographer, Peter Emerson, who first promoted photography as art in its own right. He contended that each photograph requires its own composition, free from the restrictions of formulas. In the image above, for the sake of symmetry in the design, the right is a mirror of the left.

Geikie Gorge and the Fitzroy River, Geikie Gorge National Park, the Kimberley, Western Australia.

evaluating

*Criticism, like rain, should be gentle enough to nourish
a man's growth without destroying his roots.*

Frank A. Clark – author

Evaluation of a piece of work begins as soon as the production starts, in the
very first choices made. It may be difficult to achieve, but objectivity is worth
striving for. A feel for the aesthetic values in an image develops with experience.

Cranbrook Bell, Stirling Range, Western Australia.

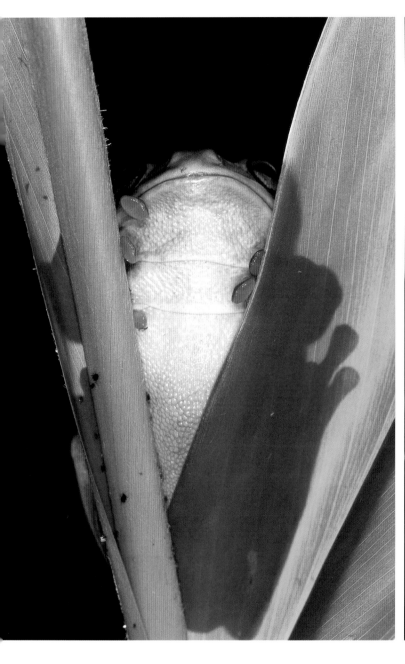

During the stages of production, a work's creator will question everything. To establish a knowledge base from which to make meaningful evaluation, it is important to view the work of others in the same field. But it is also important to trust your own knowledge and intuition.

Left to right: Green Tree-frog; Cruiser Butterfly; Green Tree-snake, Tropical North Queensland.

Above: Gulf of Carpentaria, Queensland.
Following pages: Mount Hotham, Alpine National Park, Victoria.

failure

We learn wisdom from failure much more than from success....

and probably he who never made a mistake never made a discovery.

Samuel Smiles – social and political reformer, author

Creative tasks may have numerous development phases many of which may be considered failures.

Take the opportunity to learn from failure. Look at it objectively – perhaps it is a new style of work

that needs time to germinate. What may be considered failure today could well be success tomorrow.

An Egret blur at 1/15 of a second, Kakadu National Park, Northern Territory.

Initially, I considered this image hopeless blurs, and the only reason I kept it was to illustrate what happens when the shutter speed is not set correctly. Ten years later I began to appreciate that the images did in fact capture the true spirit of the moment.

Crested Terns at 1/30 of a second, Great Barrier Reef, Queensland.

originality

We have an obligation to art and to ourselves to search for and express our own truth. Nature is a wonderful source for inspiration in terms of originality and aesthetics. How well that source is exploited depends on technical skill and creativity. Originality comes not from being first, nor best: it comes from within and requires constant striving for spiritual and mental growth.

Originality can be demonstrated in the composition and design of images and in how we use them – in choosing the method of reproduction, framing, where and how an image is printed and the purpose for which it is reproduced.

Palm forest, Mount Tamborine, Queensland.

The design of an image and the manner in which it is presented both provide innumerable opportunities to stamp the image with our own personality. Working creatively involves taking risks and venturing into non-conformity. It requires passionate commitment to pursuing personal truths. These paths are outside the comfort zone but well within the zone of excitement.

Limestone stacks, Port Campbell National Park, Victoria.

focus

Few would argue that focusing on a single outcome produces superior results. Focus on work is like meditation, allowing extraneous mental chatter to fade away, single-mindedly pursuing the task at hand. With complete concentration, a connection with the subject and the work is formed, helping us surmount barriers, break through fears and realise original work at a level never before imagined.

Left to right: Sleeping Koala; exploring Short-beaked Echidna; scratching Eastern Grey Kangaroo; all Queensland.

Patience and focus are essential in bird photography. Capturing that moment in the life of a common duck when the bird performs and the light is right can provide opportunities for considerable drama in the final production.

A Pacific Black Duck takes a bath in the Royal Botanic Gardens, Sydney, New South Wales.

Do not dwell in the past, do not dream of the future,
concentrate the mind on the present moment.

Siddhartha Buddha – founding figure of Buddhism

Above: Cradle Mountain, Cradle Mountain– Lake St Clair National Park, Tasmania.
Opposite: Mount Augustus, Mount Augustus (Burringurrah) National Park Western Australia.

resolution

When I am working on a problem, I never think about beauty, but when
I have finished, if the solution is not beautiful, I know it is wrong.

R. Buckminster Fuller – inventor, architect, engineer, mathematician

The final resolution of all the elements of a production seldom falls into place with a satisfying *click*. But when it does, there's a wonderful inner satisfaction. What keeps the creative person ever striving to produce is the occasional experience of that strong feeling, and the conviction that the pinnacle of achievement has not yet been reached.

Mudflats, King Sound, the Kimberley, Western Australia.

Each time I passed this headland over a five day period I watched from the high clifftops how the light fell during the late afternoon. On the sixth day I climbed down to make my images. I made more than sixty over three hours, but this is the only one that captured the sense of the place for me.

Above: Anson Bay, Norfolk Island, off New South Wales.
Following pages: Flinders Ranges National Park, South Australia.

compulsion

selecting

revealing

confronting

acceptance

fulfilment

The satisfaction that comes from having realised nature's inspiration into a production – a photograph, a piece of writing, a painting, a native garden – is often enhanced by sharing observations and feelings, by making a connection with others.

Each event in the creative process can be thought of as an act in a play. Each act tells of episodes in the drama and each gives the play its layers of meaning as it builds to the last act. In our dramatisation of the creative journey, while each act has its twists and turns, this last act may contain some surprising challenges as we reflect on how much of our inner selves to reveal.

Reminiscent of stage fright, such decisions will always be a challenge. But, as with stage fright, during the performance misgivings slip away with the discovery that the experience of sharing creativity not only enhances life experience but also brings understanding of the natural world, the world of which we are such an influential part.

Opposite: **When the bush is in bloom nectar feeding birds come, as if from nowhere, to feed on its bounty.**

Rainbow Lorikeet on Golden Penda, Brisbane, Queensland.

compulsion

What is it that is so compelling about sharing a creation? Some in the world of literature, music and the arts have reported that their inner compulsion has a life of its own, requiring expression but not requiring the approval of others. Still there is the drive to give their creation life by putting it in the public domain. That drive expresses itself at various levels: sharing might involve showing the family photo album to a friend or entering a photographic image in an international competition. To varying degrees, we need the approval and acceptance of others to affirm the particular and personal way we see our world, our place in the world, our judgement, our skills.

Above: The magnificent view from the Hazards to the heathlands of Wineglass Bay, Freycinet National Park, Tasmania. *Above right:* Geraldton Wax.
Opposite: Coastal heathland grass-trees, Kalbarri National Park, Western Australia.

Experiencing the natural wonders of the Great Barrier Reef is such a profound experience that most people want to share it with others. Making a visual record is the most popular way of doing that. Interestingly, diving the reef is not an experience that is easily expressed because it is such an alien world and making images of its denizens presents unique challenges. The Coral Trout opposite, normally marauding carnivores, are hanging out beneath a cavern waiting for the late afternoon when they are more inclined to hunt. Stalking and photographing fish has been my driving force for more than forty years. Perhaps more than most environments, the underwater world is so dramatic that it commands that each encounter be shared.

Above: Wreck Island, one of the many alluring islands in the Capricorn Bunker Group, Great Barrier Reef Marine Park and World Heritage Area, Queensland.

Opposite: Coral Trout, Great Barrier Reef Marine Park and World Heritage Area, Queensland.

Following pages: Hopetoun Falls, Otway Ranges, Victoria.

selecting

The selection process lies at the heart of who we are and how we connect. In selecting what others may view, the potential for collision between the internal and external worlds becomes obvious. Selection criteria and parameters for sharing must be established; personal motivations examined; ego confronted; audience defined; and sensibilities prepared for critical feedback.

The striking Boab, a challenge in the selection of the shape that has most appeal; the Kimberley, Western Australia.

Affecting people to the degree that they are compelled to stop, look and consider a piece of work is a challenge, particularly in this multimedia age when we are bombarded with so much visual information. When selecting work for showing, explore your reasons for connecting with others and be guided in the selection by personal truth.

There are many and varied selection criteria, depending on medium and subject. Are birds selected using the same criteria as for flowers? Is colour, shape, texture, or form the major influence? Can you trust your own judgement? And does it matter what other people think? This is where we need to examine our motives: what do we hope to gain from showing our creative work?

Above, left to right: Scarlet Banksia, Finke River Mallee, Long-style Grevillea.

Images draw people under their spell for a number of reasons. It could be colour, texture, patterning, or design. Or an image may bring to mind something special to the viewer; something the image evokes that may, in fact, have little to do with the actual subject of the picture.

Above, left to right: Male Scarlet-chested Parrot, western Queensland; male Regent Bowerbird, south-east Queensland; male Little Lorikeet, south-east Queensland.

revealing

*If you reveal your secrets to the wind, you should
not blame the wind for revealing them to the trees.*

Kahlil Gibran – poet, philosopher, artist

In all cultures, creative pursuits such as dance, art and story-telling lie at the heart of the community. My culture does not stipulate who may express themselves and their culture through art and in what medium. Australian Aborigines are selective about who can tell and receive their stories and in what medium. Goyma is a six-year-old from Elco Island off the Arnhem Land coast. Because he is the child of senior community members, Goyma will be taught the language and traditions of his people, and will be privy to stories that will not be revealed to other community members.

Above and opposite: Florence Falls, Litchfield National Park, Northern Territory.

On a visit to the traditional lands of Aṉangu at Uluṟu, you might be fortunate enough to be present when the land's custodians share age-old stories through dance, art and story-telling. The kinds of stories and the depth and detail in which they may be told are approved by the elders as being appropriate for non-Aṉangu to witness and hear.

For entirely different reasons, you may experience a similar selectivity when you choose with whom and in what depth and detail you will reveal your feelings in relating your stories to others. You may be comfortable sharing intimate feelings with those you trust, but feel guarded when connecting with the broader community.

Uluṟu, Uluṟu–Kata Tjuṯa National Park, Northern Territory.

Both these landscapes are special and it is in such places that a spiritual connection to the land is likely to be felt. People who experience that connection may share their personal stories verbally, in writing or through some other medium such as photography. Some of what is shared will relate to the special place, while some will be more revealing of the person sharing.

Left: Mount Wellington, Hobart, Tasmania.
Right: The Pinnacles in Nambung National Park, Western Australia.

confronting

Heroes take journeys, confront dragons,
and discover the treasure of their true selves.

Carol Pearson – author, leadership coach

In the natural world are many situations that arouse irrational fears – of being alone in a wild place, of dark places, of wild animals, or of open spaces. Acquiring knowledge that leads to understanding will rationalise the irrational. By extension, fear of presenting creative work to be criticised can also be overcome. Confronting the object of fear may not only neutralise the fear, but also open doors to exciting new worlds.

Above: Many people fear snakes yet few are dangerous. A python may bite, but has no venom. Carpet Python, New South Wales.
Opposite: Overcoming fear of drowning provides opportunities to enter worlds undreamed of. Great Barrier Reef, Queensland.
Following pages: Being alone in a wild place can be confronting, but it is a wonderfully rewarding experience. Cape Tribulation, Queensland.

acceptance

At the heart of personality is the need to feel a sense of being lovable without having to qualify for that acceptance.

Dr Paul Tournier – medical practitioner, counsellor

Rejection is always painful: a first reaction is a feeling of failure. Perhaps, quite to the contrary, it is an opportunity for growth. Examine your motives and the connections you were attempting. Were you doing your best? Did you meet the criteria? Are you being realistic? It is a struggle. There is a reason for everything, and understanding can help turn negative to positive. In the field, I am only now, after forty years, starting to accept, without experiencing feelings of frustration, what I cannot change, such as the weather conditions, encounters as they occur – hard lessons but well worth learning.

Dawn light on a dreary overcast morning – volcanic rocks washed smooth by pounding seas at Norfolk Island, off the New South Wales coast.

Sometimes even the simplest subjects can produce stunning pictures.

Above left: Carried by a forest stream this eucalypt leaf's journey is briefly interrupted by a protruding rock. Carnarvon National Park, Queensland

Above centre: A Flannel Flower, floral symbol in New South Wales of the centenary of Federation (2001), makes up for its lack of dramatic colour by the elegance of its form.

Above right: A dragonfly pauses briefly on a twig above a stream. Kakadu National Park, Northern Territory.

The keys to acceptance are patience and faith. When they are blended with knowledge and understanding, anything is possible.

Above: The Tully River on a typically wet day, Tropical North Queensland.

Opposite: Pied Imperial-Pigeon, Tropical North Queensland.

fulfilment

I believe that the very purpose of our life is to seek happiness. That is clear. Whether one believes in religion or not, whether one believes in this religion or that religion, we all are seeking something better in life. So, I think, the very motion of our life is towards happiness.

Dalai Lama – Tibetan spiritual leader, Buddhism

If I have learned one thing in my life, it would be that the natural world can provide, not just the air we breathe, the water we drink and the ground we stand on, but also our mental and spiritual wellbeing. I have also learned how important connecting with nature (including humanity) is in our overall development as thinking, feeling, spiritual beings. We reflect ourselves through nature in creative activity and can learn who we are, and where we belong in the world. Then we can begin to feel connected, fulfilled and happy.

Above: Fuchsia Heath, New South Wales. *Opposite:* MacKenzie Falls, Grampians National Park, Victoria.
Following pages: Kata Tjuṯa, Uluṟu–Kata Tjuṯa National Park, Northern Territory.
Followed by: Wategos Beach, Byron Bay, New South Wales.

Feather of a Pheasant Coucal, Bunitj Clan Estate during Gudjewg (wet season), Kakadu National Park, Northern Territory.

I feel it with my body

with my blood

feeling all these trees

all this country.

When this wind blow

you feel it.

Same for country....

You feel it.

You can look

but feeling...

that make you.

The late Big Bill Neidjie, OAM

Respected Senior Elder of the Gagudju Community
and a traditional owner of the Bunitj estate in northern Kakadu,
who asked that his name be used after his passing to help
with the preservation of his people's culture.

index

behind the photographs

The photographs in this book were taken throughout my career (1966 to 2004), although most are recently taken. The images represent the inspirations that nature has offered me, and reflect the many frames of mind in which I approach image-making.

Taken under every conceivable condition Australia can offer – in the air and on land, from the desert to beneath the sea, on fine sunny days and in the midst of violent storms – the images are produced from the palette of Australia, seen through this photographer's eyes.

www.photographaustralia.com.au

Creating this book has taken me on a wonderful journey. It has been my most challenging project to date. I hope that in the images you can read something of my experiences. Perhaps they bring to mind an experience of yours. If so, share it with us through www.photographaustralia.com.au, a free community photographic e-zine.

www.steveparishexhibits.com.au

Many of the images in this book are available as limited edition prints online at www.steveparishexhibits.com.au.

Small format photography

I use small format 35 mm Nikon cameras for plants and animals, and for opportunistic landscape images that may present. The high speed auto focus, light weight, very long lenses and high speed motor driven film capabilities for action photography make them perfect for wildlife. Modern 35 mm cameras also have metering systems for situations such as a bird flying through the exposure ranges that may vary up to 5 f-stops which would be impossible to calculate manually. I also use 35 mm Nikon cameras underwater, although many of the images from deeper southern waters were taken with a medium format Hasselblad camera using very high quality lenses.

Medium format photography

For enlargement clarity I use medium format 6 x 7 cm Mamiya 2 rangefinder cameras with wide-angle lenses, Mamiya RZ reflex cameras for long lens work, and a Fuji 6 x 17 cm panoramic camera. This format is good for landscape photography on the ground and in the air, although I also use this format for medium close-ups of plants and landscape detail, particularly where major enlargement is required for prints.

The film

The film stock used to produce most of the images was Ektachrome VS ISO 100 and Velvia ISO 50 and 100.

Video

In addition to still photography, I shoot digital video with a Canon XL1. This footage is forming part of a library for the production of DVDs.

acknowledgements

A very special thanks to Catherine Prentice, who worked closely with me on the development of the text and the structure of this book. Her patience with the numerous re-writes and re-edits of images was a major factor in this book's difficult evolution. I would also like to thank Ann Wright, Kate Lovett and Deb and Ed Shapiro for their generosity with critical suggestions for the text. Thanks must also go to my old and dear friend, nature photographer and naturalist, Ian Morris, who, while working on a book on his beloved frogs and snakes in an adjoining room, always made himself available when I was confronted with difficult image selection decisions. I am grateful, too, to my friends and colleagues, Allan Fox and Peter Slater, for their encouragement with this challenging project.

A special thanks also for the enormous effort made by the staff of Colour Chiefs Digital Imaging who produced the digital scans for printing.

We invite you to visit the Steve Parish Publishing websites where you can view Steve's wide range of products and participate in Australia's only photographic e-zine.

online

FOR PRODUCTS
www.steveparish.com.au

View books, calendars, diaries, children's books, stationery and gifts.

FOR LIMITED EDITION PRINTS
www.steveparishexhibits.com.au

View a selection of wildlife, wildflower and landscape photographs with options for framing and purchase.

FOR PHOTOGRAPHY EZINE
www.photographaustralia.com.au

Join discussions on photographing Australia, photo tips, photo locations, competitions, freebies, and more.

Text, photography and photographic design: Steve Parish

Cover design: Elise Butler

While every effort was made to find copyright holders of material quoted, some were not able to be traced. The Publisher would be pleased to hear from copyright holders and rectify any omissions. Albert Einstein quoted with permission of the Albert Einstein Archives, Hebrew University of Jerusalem, Israel. The Dalai Lama quoted with permission granted through Ed and Deb Shapiro. R. Buckminster Fuller quoted courtesy, the Estate of R. Buckminster Fuller.

Printed in China by Printplus Ltd

Film by Colour Chiefs Digital Imaging, Australia

Produced at the Steve Parish Publishing Studios, Australia